# 50 Northern Comfort Recipes for Home

By: Kelly Johnson

# Table of Contents

- Maple Glazed Pork Tenderloin
- Creamy Potato Leek Soup
- Classic Beef Stew
- Honey Mustard Roasted Chicken
- Savory Stuffed Bell Peppers
- Herb-Crusted Lamb Chops
- Wild Mushroom Risotto
- Baked Cod with Lemon Butter
- Spiced Apple Cider Roast
- Garlic Mashed Potatoes
- Cranberry Orange Glazed Ham
- Butternut Squash and Sage Soup
- Chicken Pot Pie
- Apple Cinnamon Pancakes
- Rustic Shepherd's Pie
- Spinach and Feta Stuffed Chicken
- Sweet Potato and Black Bean Chili
- Classic Beef Stroganoff
- Blueberry Lemon Muffins
- Creamy Tomato Basil Soup
- Maple Pecan Carrots
- Roasted Brussels Sprouts with Bacon
- Beef and Barley Soup
- Raspberry Almond Cake
- Garlic Parmesan Roasted Potatoes
- Chicken and Mushroom Casserole
- Pumpkin Spice Bread
- Buttermilk Biscuits
- Roasted Vegetable Medley
- Cranberry Walnut Salad
- Creamy Broccoli Cheddar Soup
- Herb-Infused Roast Beef
- Pumpkin Risotto
- Spaghetti Squash with Marinara Sauce
- Apple Harvest Salad
- Cornbread Stuffing

- Chicken Marsala
- Pecan-Crusted Salmon
- Maple-Glazed Carrots
- Beef and Vegetable Skewers
- Garlic Butter Shrimp
- Gingerbread Cookies
- Creamy Spinach Artichoke Dip
- Chicken and Rice Soup
- Blackberry Cobbler
- Sausage and Potato Hash
- Roasted Tomato and Basil Bruschetta
- Chocolate Chip Walnut Cookies
- Spiced Pear Compote
- Savory Herb Scones

**Maple Glazed Pork Tenderloin**

**Ingredients:**

- 1.5 lbs pork tenderloin
- 1/2 cup pure maple syrup
- 1/4 cup Dijon mustard
- 2 tbsp soy sauce
- 2 tbsp olive oil
- 2 cloves garlic, minced
- 1 tsp dried thyme
- 1/2 tsp ground black pepper
- 1/2 tsp salt

**Instructions:**

1. **Preheat Oven:** Preheat your oven to 375°F (190°C).
2. **Prepare Glaze:** In a small bowl, mix together the maple syrup, Dijon mustard, soy sauce, olive oil, minced garlic, dried thyme, black pepper, and salt.
3. **Prepare Pork:** Trim any silver skin from the pork tenderloin. Season the tenderloin with salt and pepper.
4. **Sear Pork:** Heat a skillet over medium-high heat. Add a small amount of oil, then sear the pork tenderloin on all sides until browned, about 2-3 minutes per side.
5. **Glaze Pork:** Brush the pork tenderloin generously with the maple glaze mixture.
6. **Bake:** Transfer the seared pork tenderloin to a baking dish. Pour any remaining glaze over the top of the pork. Bake in the preheated oven for 20-25 minutes, or until the internal temperature reaches 145°F (63°C).
7. **Rest:** Remove the pork tenderloin from the oven and let it rest for 5 minutes before slicing.
8. **Serve:** Slice the pork tenderloin and serve with your choice of sides. Drizzle any remaining glaze from the baking dish over the slices.

**Creamy Potato Leek Soup**

**Ingredients:**

- 4 large leeks, white and light green parts only, cleaned and sliced
- 3 tbsp unsalted butter
- 4 cups peeled and diced potatoes (about 4 medium potatoes)
- 4 cups chicken or vegetable broth
- 1 cup heavy cream
- 1 cup milk
- 2 cloves garlic, minced
- 1 tsp dried thyme
- 1 bay leaf
- Salt and pepper to taste
- Fresh chives or parsley, chopped (for garnish)

**Instructions:**

1. **Prepare Leeks:** In a large pot, melt the butter over medium heat. Add the sliced leeks and cook, stirring occasionally, until softened and translucent, about 5-7 minutes.
2. **Add Garlic:** Add the minced garlic and cook for another minute, until fragrant.
3. **Add Potatoes and Broth:** Stir in the diced potatoes, chicken or vegetable broth, dried thyme, and bay leaf. Bring to a boil.
4. **Simmer:** Reduce the heat and let the soup simmer until the potatoes are tender, about 15-20 minutes.
5. **Blend Soup:** Remove the bay leaf. Use an immersion blender to blend the soup until smooth, or carefully transfer to a blender in batches.
6. **Add Cream and Milk:** Stir in the heavy cream and milk. Heat the soup over low heat until warmed through. Season with salt and pepper to taste.
7. **Serve:** Ladle the soup into bowls and garnish with chopped chives or parsley.
8. **Enjoy:** Serve hot with crusty bread or your favorite soup accompaniment.

**Classic Beef Stew**

**Ingredients:**

- 2 lbs beef chuck, cut into 1-inch cubes
- 3 tbsp vegetable oil
- 1 large onion, chopped
- 3 cloves garlic, minced
- 4 cups beef broth
- 1 cup red wine (optional, can substitute with more beef broth)
- 4 large carrots, peeled and sliced
- 3 large potatoes, peeled and diced
- 2 stalks celery, chopped
- 2 tbsp tomato paste
- 1 tbsp Worcestershire sauce
- 1 tsp dried thyme
- 1 bay leaf
- 1 cup frozen peas
- Salt and pepper to taste
- 2 tbsp all-purpose flour (for thickening)
- 2 tbsp water (for thickening)

**Instructions:**

1. **Brown Beef:** Heat the vegetable oil in a large pot or Dutch oven over medium-high heat. Add the beef cubes in batches and brown on all sides. Remove and set aside.
2. **Cook Aromatics:** In the same pot, add the chopped onion and cook until softened, about 5 minutes. Add the minced garlic and cook for another minute.
3. **Deglaze:** Stir in the tomato paste and cook for 1-2 minutes. Pour in the red wine (if using) and scrape up any browned bits from the bottom of the pot.
4. **Add Beef and Broth:** Return the browned beef to the pot. Add the beef broth, Worcestershire sauce, dried thyme, and bay leaf. Bring to a boil.
5. **Simmer:** Reduce the heat to low, cover, and let the stew simmer for 1 hour.
6. **Add Vegetables:** Add the carrots, potatoes, and celery. Continue to simmer for another 30-45 minutes, until the beef and vegetables are tender.
7. **Thicken Stew:** In a small bowl, mix the flour and water to form a slurry. Stir the slurry into the stew and cook for an additional 5-10 minutes, until the stew thickens.
8. **Add Peas:** Stir in the frozen peas and cook for another 5 minutes. Season with salt and pepper to taste.
9. **Serve:** Remove the bay leaf before serving. Ladle the stew into bowls and enjoy hot with crusty bread or over rice.

# Honey Mustard Roasted Chicken

## Ingredients:

- 1 whole chicken (about 4-5 lbs)
- 1/4 cup honey
- 1/4 cup Dijon mustard
- 2 tbsp whole grain mustard
- 3 tbsp olive oil
- 3 cloves garlic, minced
- 1 tbsp fresh thyme leaves (or 1 tsp dried thyme)
- 1 tsp paprika
- Salt and pepper to taste
- 1 lemon, quartered
- 1 onion, quartered
- Fresh thyme sprigs (for garnish)

## Instructions:

1. **Preheat Oven:** Preheat your oven to 425°F (220°C).
2. **Prepare Glaze:** In a bowl, whisk together the honey, Dijon mustard, whole grain mustard, olive oil, minced garlic, fresh thyme, paprika, salt, and pepper.
3. **Prepare Chicken:** Remove the giblets from the chicken and pat it dry with paper towels. Place the chicken in a roasting pan or on a rack set over a baking sheet.
4. **Season Chicken:** Rub the honey mustard mixture all over the chicken, including under the skin where possible. Place the lemon and onion quarters inside the cavity of the chicken.
5. **Roast Chicken:** Roast the chicken in the preheated oven for 1 to 1.5 hours, or until the internal temperature reaches 165°F (74°C) and the skin is golden and crispy. Baste the chicken occasionally with the pan juices.
6. **Rest Chicken:** Remove the chicken from the oven and let it rest for 10-15 minutes before carving. This helps the juices redistribute.
7. **Garnish and Serve:** Garnish with fresh thyme sprigs if desired. Serve the chicken with your favorite sides and enjoy!

**Savory Stuffed Bell Peppers**

**Ingredients:**

- 4 large bell peppers (any color)
- 1 lb ground beef or ground turkey
- 1 cup cooked rice (white, brown, or wild rice)
- 1 small onion, finely chopped
- 2 cloves garlic, minced
- 1 cup tomato sauce
- 1 cup shredded cheddar cheese
- 1 tsp dried oregano
- 1 tsp dried basil
- 1/2 tsp paprika
- Salt and pepper to taste
- 2 tbsp olive oil
- Fresh parsley or basil for garnish (optional)

**Instructions:**

1. **Preheat Oven:** Preheat your oven to 375°F (190°C).
2. **Prepare Peppers:** Cut the tops off the bell peppers and remove the seeds and membranes. Set aside.
3. **Cook Filling:** Heat the olive oil in a skillet over medium heat. Add the chopped onion and cook until softened, about 5 minutes. Add the minced garlic and cook for another minute.
4. **Brown Meat:** Add the ground beef or turkey to the skillet and cook until browned, breaking it up with a spoon. Drain any excess fat.
5. **Combine Ingredients:** Stir in the cooked rice, tomato sauce, shredded cheese, dried oregano, dried basil, paprika, salt, and pepper. Mix until well combined and heated through.
6. **Stuff Peppers:** Spoon the filling into each bell pepper, packing it down gently. Place the stuffed peppers upright in a baking dish.
7. **Bake Peppers:** Cover the baking dish with aluminum foil and bake for 30 minutes. Remove the foil and bake for an additional 10-15 minutes, until the peppers are tender and the tops are slightly browned.
8. **Garnish and Serve:** Garnish with fresh parsley or basil if desired. Serve hot.

Enjoy your savory stuffed bell peppers!

# Herb-Crusted Lamb Chops

## Ingredients:

- 8 lamb chops (about 1-inch thick)
- 1/4 cup fresh rosemary leaves, finely chopped
- 1/4 cup fresh thyme leaves, finely chopped
- 1/4 cup fresh parsley, finely chopped
- 3 cloves garlic, minced
- 1/2 cup breadcrumbs (panko or regular)
- 1/4 cup grated Parmesan cheese
- 1/4 cup Dijon mustard
- 2 tbsp olive oil
- Salt and pepper to taste
- Lemon wedges (for serving)

## Instructions:

1. **Preheat Oven:** Preheat your oven to 400°F (200°C).
2. **Prepare Herb Mixture:** In a bowl, mix together the rosemary, thyme, parsley, minced garlic, breadcrumbs, and Parmesan cheese.
3. **Season Lamb:** Season the lamb chops with salt and pepper on both sides. Brush each chop with Dijon mustard, coating them evenly.
4. **Coat with Herbs:** Press the herb mixture onto the mustard-coated lamb chops, ensuring a good, even crust.
5. **Sear Chops:** Heat the olive oil in a large oven-proof skillet over medium-high heat. Sear the lamb chops for about 2 minutes per side, until browned.
6. **Bake Chops:** Transfer the skillet to the preheated oven. Bake the lamb chops for 8-10 minutes, or until the internal temperature reaches 135°F (57°C) for medium-rare, or longer if desired.
7. **Rest and Serve:** Remove the skillet from the oven and let the lamb chops rest for 5 minutes. Serve with lemon wedges on the side.

Enjoy your flavorful and herbaceous lamb chops!

**Wild Mushroom Risotto**

**Ingredients:**

- 1 cup Arborio rice
- 1/2 cup white wine
- 4 cups chicken or vegetable broth (kept warm)
- 2 tbsp olive oil
- 1 small onion, finely chopped
- 3 cloves garlic, minced
- 2 cups mixed wild mushrooms (e.g., shiitake, cremini, porcini), cleaned and sliced
- 1/2 cup grated Parmesan cheese
- 2 tbsp unsalted butter
- 1/4 cup fresh parsley, chopped
- Salt and pepper to taste

**Instructions:**

1. **Prepare Broth:** In a saucepan, keep the chicken or vegetable broth warm over low heat.
2. **Cook Mushrooms:** In a large skillet, heat 1 tablespoon of olive oil over medium heat. Add the sliced mushrooms and cook until they are tender and browned, about 5-7 minutes. Season with a pinch of salt and pepper. Set aside.
3. **Sauté Aromatics:** In a separate large pot or Dutch oven, heat the remaining tablespoon of olive oil over medium heat. Add the chopped onion and cook until softened, about 5 minutes. Add the minced garlic and cook for another minute.
4. **Add Rice:** Stir in the Arborio rice and cook for 1-2 minutes until the rice is lightly toasted and coated with the oil.
5. **Deglaze:** Pour in the white wine and stir until it is mostly absorbed by the rice.
6. **Add Broth:** Begin adding the warm broth to the rice, one ladleful at a time, stirring frequently. Allow each addition to be absorbed before adding the next ladleful. Continue this process for about 18-20 minutes, or until the rice is creamy and cooked to al dente.
7. **Combine Ingredients:** Stir in the cooked mushrooms, Parmesan cheese, and butter. Adjust seasoning with salt and pepper to taste. Continue to cook for an additional 2-3 minutes until the cheese and butter are melted and incorporated.
8. **Garnish and Serve:** Remove from heat and stir in the chopped parsley. Serve hot, garnished with extra Parmesan cheese if desired.

Enjoy your creamy and flavorful wild mushroom risotto!

## Baked Cod with Lemon Butter

### Ingredients:

- 4 cod fillets (about 6 oz each)
- 1/4 cup unsalted butter, melted
- 2 tbsp lemon juice (freshly squeezed)
- 2 cloves garlic, minced
- 1 tsp dried thyme or 1 tbsp fresh thyme leaves
- 1 tsp dried parsley or 1 tbsp fresh parsley, chopped
- 1/2 tsp paprika
- Salt and pepper to taste
- Lemon slices (for garnish)
- Fresh parsley (for garnish)

### Instructions:

1. **Preheat Oven:** Preheat your oven to 400°F (200°C).
2. **Prepare Baking Dish:** Lightly grease a baking dish or line it with parchment paper.
3. **Mix Lemon Butter:** In a small bowl, combine the melted butter, lemon juice, minced garlic, dried thyme, dried parsley, paprika, salt, and pepper.
4. **Season Cod:** Pat the cod fillets dry with paper towels. Place them in the prepared baking dish. Brush each fillet generously with the lemon butter mixture.
5. **Bake Cod:** Bake in the preheated oven for 12-15 minutes, or until the cod is opaque and flakes easily with a fork.
6. **Garnish and Serve:** Garnish with lemon slices and fresh parsley. Serve with your choice of side dishes, such as steamed vegetables, rice, or potatoes.

Enjoy your delicious and tangy baked cod with lemon butter!

## Spiced Apple Cider Roast

**Ingredients:**

- 3-4 lbs pork loin or pork shoulder
- 2 cups apple cider
- 1/2 cup chicken or vegetable broth
- 1/4 cup brown sugar
- 2 tbsp Dijon mustard
- 2 tbsp olive oil
- 1 large onion, chopped
- 3 cloves garlic, minced
- 1 tsp ground cinnamon
- 1/2 tsp ground cloves
- 1/2 tsp ground nutmeg
- 1/2 tsp dried thyme
- 1/2 tsp dried rosemary
- Salt and pepper to taste
- 2 apples, cored and sliced
- Fresh thyme or rosemary for garnish (optional)

**Instructions:**

1. **Preheat Oven:** Preheat your oven to 350°F (175°C).
2. **Prepare Pork:** Pat the pork roast dry with paper towels. Season generously with salt and pepper.
3. **Sear Pork:** In a large oven-proof skillet or roasting pan, heat the olive oil over medium-high heat. Sear the pork roast on all sides until browned, about 4-5 minutes per side. Remove the pork from the skillet and set aside.
4. **Cook Aromatics:** In the same skillet, add the chopped onion and cook until softened, about 5 minutes. Add the minced garlic and cook for another minute.
5. **Add Spices and Liquid:** Stir in the brown sugar, Dijon mustard, cinnamon, cloves, nutmeg, dried thyme, and dried rosemary. Cook for 1-2 minutes until the sugar is dissolved. Pour in the apple cider and broth, stirring to combine.
6. **Roast Pork:** Return the seared pork roast to the skillet. Arrange the apple slices around the pork. Bring the liquid to a simmer.
7. **Bake:** Transfer the skillet or roasting pan to the preheated oven. Roast for 1.5 to 2 hours, or until the pork reaches an internal temperature of 145°F (63°C) and is tender. Baste the pork occasionally with the pan juices.
8. **Rest and Serve:** Remove the pork from the oven and let it rest for 10 minutes before slicing. Garnish with fresh thyme or rosemary if desired.

Serve with the apples and pan sauce over the top. Enjoy your flavorful and spiced apple cider roast!

**Garlic Mashed Potatoes**

**Ingredients:**

- 2 lbs russet or Yukon Gold potatoes, peeled and cut into chunks
- 4 cloves garlic, peeled
- 1/2 cup milk (whole or 2%)
- 1/4 cup unsalted butter
- Salt and pepper to taste
- 2 tbsp fresh parsley, chopped (optional, for garnish)

**Instructions:**

1. **Cook Potatoes and Garlic:** In a large pot, combine the potatoes and garlic. Cover with cold water and add a pinch of salt. Bring to a boil over high heat, then reduce heat and simmer until the potatoes are tender, about 15-20 minutes.
2. **Drain:** Drain the potatoes and garlic well and return them to the pot.
3. **Mash:** Using a potato masher or a ricer, mash the potatoes and garlic until smooth.
4. **Add Butter and Milk:** In a small saucepan, heat the milk and butter until the butter is melted and the milk is warm. Pour this mixture into the mashed potatoes and stir until combined and creamy. Adjust the consistency by adding more milk if needed.
5. **Season:** Season with salt and pepper to taste. Mix well.
6. **Garnish and Serve:** Transfer the mashed potatoes to a serving dish. Garnish with fresh parsley if desired. Serve hot.

Enjoy your creamy, garlic-infused mashed potatoes!

**Cranberry Orange Glazed Ham**

**Ingredients:**

- 1 fully cooked bone-in ham (about 8-10 lbs)
- 1 cup cranberry sauce (homemade or canned)
- 1/2 cup orange juice
- 1/4 cup honey
- 2 tbsp Dijon mustard
- 1/4 cup brown sugar
- 1/2 tsp ground cinnamon
- 1/4 tsp ground cloves
- 1/4 tsp ground allspice
- 2 tbsp cornstarch (optional, for thickening)
- 2 tbsp water (optional, for cornstarch slurry)

**Instructions:**

1. **Preheat Oven:** Preheat your oven to 325°F (165°C).
2. **Prepare Ham:** Place the ham in a roasting pan, cut side down. Score the surface of the ham in a diamond pattern.
3. **Make Glaze:** In a saucepan, combine the cranberry sauce, orange juice, honey, Dijon mustard, brown sugar, cinnamon, cloves, and allspice. Cook over medium heat, stirring occasionally, until the mixture is smooth and slightly thickened, about 5-7 minutes.
4. **Apply Glaze:** Brush some of the glaze over the surface of the ham, ensuring it gets into the scored areas.
5. **Bake Ham:** Cover the roasting pan loosely with aluminum foil and bake in the preheated oven for 1.5 to 2 hours, or until the internal temperature of the ham reaches 140°F (60°C).
6. **Glaze Ham:** Remove the foil, brush the ham with more glaze, and return to the oven. Bake for an additional 20-30 minutes, basting with the glaze every 10 minutes, until the glaze is caramelized and the ham is heated through.
7. **Thicken Glaze (Optional):** If you prefer a thicker glaze, dissolve the cornstarch in water to make a slurry and stir it into the remaining glaze. Cook for an additional 2-3 minutes until thickened.
8. **Rest and Serve:** Let the ham rest for 10-15 minutes before carving. Serve with extra cranberry orange glaze on the side.

Enjoy your flavorful and festive cranberry orange glazed ham!

# Butternut Squash and Sage Soup

## Ingredients:

- 1 large butternut squash (about 2 lbs), peeled, seeded, and cubed
- 1 large onion, chopped
- 2 cloves garlic, minced
- 2 tbsp olive oil
- 4 cups vegetable or chicken broth
- 1/2 cup coconut milk or heavy cream
- 1 tsp dried sage (or 1 tbsp fresh sage, chopped)
- 1/2 tsp ground nutmeg
- Salt and pepper to taste
- Fresh sage leaves for garnish (optional)

## Instructions:

1. **Prepare Squash:** Preheat your oven to 400°F (200°C). Spread the butternut squash cubes on a baking sheet, drizzle with 1 tablespoon of olive oil, and season with salt and pepper. Roast for 25-30 minutes, or until the squash is tender and lightly caramelized.
2. **Cook Aromatics:** In a large pot, heat the remaining tablespoon of olive oil over medium heat. Add the chopped onion and cook until softened, about 5 minutes. Add the minced garlic and cook for an additional 1 minute.
3. **Combine Ingredients:** Add the roasted butternut squash to the pot. Stir in the broth, coconut milk, dried sage, and ground nutmeg. Bring to a boil, then reduce the heat and simmer for 10 minutes.
4. **Blend Soup:** Use an immersion blender to puree the soup until smooth. Alternatively, transfer the soup in batches to a blender and blend until smooth. Return the soup to the pot if using a blender.
5. **Season and Serve:** Taste the soup and adjust seasoning with salt and pepper as needed. Heat through if necessary.
6. **Garnish:** Ladle the soup into bowls and garnish with fresh sage leaves if desired.

Enjoy your creamy and comforting butternut squash and sage soup!

**Chicken Pot Pie**

**Ingredients:**

- **For the Filling:**
    - 2 cups cooked chicken, diced (e.g., rotisserie chicken or leftover roast chicken)
    - 1 cup carrots, diced
    - 1 cup frozen peas
    - 1 cup potatoes, diced
    - 1/2 cup celery, diced
    - 1/2 cup onion, chopped
    - 2 cloves garlic, minced
    - 1/4 cup all-purpose flour
    - 1 cup chicken broth
    - 1 cup milk or heavy cream
    - 1/2 tsp dried thyme
    - 1/2 tsp dried rosemary
    - Salt and pepper to taste
    - 2 tbsp unsalted butter
- **For the Crust:**
    - 1 package of pre-made pie crusts (or homemade if preferred)
    - 1 egg, beaten (for egg wash)

**Instructions:**

1. **Preheat Oven:** Preheat your oven to 425°F (220°C).
2. **Cook Vegetables:** In a large skillet or saucepan, melt the butter over medium heat. Add the onions, garlic, celery, and carrots. Cook until softened, about 5-7 minutes.
3. **Make the Sauce:** Stir in the flour and cook for 1-2 minutes until the mixture is lightly golden. Gradually add the chicken broth and milk, stirring continuously to avoid lumps. Cook until the mixture thickens and becomes creamy, about 5 minutes.
4. **Combine Ingredients:** Add the cooked chicken, peas, potatoes, thyme, rosemary, salt, and pepper to the sauce. Stir to combine and heat through.
5. **Assemble Pie:** Roll out one of the pie crusts and fit it into a 9-inch pie dish. Pour the chicken filling into the pie crust.
6. **Top with Crust:** Roll out the second pie crust and place it over the filling. Trim and crimp the edges to seal. Cut a few slits in the top crust to allow steam to escape. Brush the top crust with the beaten egg for a golden finish.
7. **Bake:** Bake in the preheated oven for 30-35 minutes, or until the crust is golden brown and the filling is bubbly.
8. **Cool and Serve:** Let the pot pie cool for about 10 minutes before serving to allow the filling to set.

Enjoy your classic and comforting chicken pot pie!

# Apple Cinnamon Pancakes

**Ingredients:**

- **For the Pancake Batter:**
    - 1 1/2 cups all-purpose flour
    - 2 tbsp granulated sugar
    - 1 tbsp baking powder
    - 1/2 tsp salt
    - 1/2 tsp ground cinnamon
    - 1 1/4 cups milk
    - 1 large egg
    - 2 tbsp unsalted butter, melted
    - 1 tsp vanilla extract
- **For the Apple Topping:**
    - 2 medium apples, peeled, cored, and diced
    - 2 tbsp unsalted butter
    - 1/4 cup brown sugar
    - 1/2 tsp ground cinnamon
    - 1/4 tsp ground nutmeg
    - 1/4 cup water
- **Optional Garnishes:**
    - Maple syrup
    - Powdered sugar
    - Whipped cream

**Instructions:**

1. **Prepare Apple Topping:**
    - In a medium skillet, melt the butter over medium heat. Add the diced apples and cook for 3-4 minutes until they begin to soften.
    - Stir in the brown sugar, cinnamon, nutmeg, and water. Cook for an additional 5-7 minutes, or until the apples are tender and the mixture has thickened slightly. Remove from heat and set aside.
2. **Make Pancake Batter:**
    - In a large bowl, whisk together the flour, sugar, baking powder, salt, and cinnamon.
    - In another bowl, mix the milk, egg, melted butter, and vanilla extract until well combined.
    - Pour the wet ingredients into the dry ingredients and stir until just combined. The batter should be slightly lumpy. Do not overmix.
3. **Cook Pancakes:**
    - Heat a griddle or non-stick skillet over medium heat and lightly grease with butter or oil.

       - Pour 1/4 cup of batter onto the griddle for each pancake. Cook until bubbles form on the surface and the edges look set, about 2-3 minutes. Flip and cook until golden brown on the other side, about 1-2 minutes more.
4. **Serve:**
       - Serve the pancakes warm with a generous spoonful of the apple topping on top.
       - Optional: Drizzle with maple syrup, sprinkle with powdered sugar, or add a dollop of whipped cream if desired.

Enjoy your delicious apple cinnamon pancakes!

# Rustic Shepherd's Pie

## Ingredients:

- **For the Filling:**
    - 1 lb ground beef or lamb
    - 1 medium onion, chopped
    - 2 cloves garlic, minced
    - 2 medium carrots, diced
    - 1 cup frozen peas
    - 1 cup beef or chicken broth
    - 1 tbsp tomato paste
    - 1 tbsp Worcestershire sauce
    - 1 tsp dried thyme
    - 1 tsp dried rosemary
    - Salt and pepper to taste
    - 2 tbsp olive oil
- **For the Mashed Potato Topping:**
    - 2 lbs potatoes, peeled and cubed
    - 1/4 cup milk (whole or 2%)
    - 1/4 cup unsalted butter
    - Salt and pepper to taste

## Instructions:

1. **Prepare Mashed Potatoes:**
    - In a large pot, cover the potatoes with cold water and add a pinch of salt. Bring to a boil and cook until the potatoes are tender, about 15-20 minutes.
    - Drain the potatoes and return them to the pot. Mash with milk and butter until smooth. Season with salt and pepper. Set aside.
2. **Make the Filling:**
    - In a large skillet or sauté pan, heat the olive oil over medium heat. Add the chopped onion and cook until softened, about 5 minutes.
    - Add the minced garlic and cook for an additional 1 minute.
    - Add the ground beef or lamb, breaking it up with a spoon, and cook until browned and cooked through, about 8 minutes. Drain any excess fat if necessary.
    - Stir in the diced carrots, peas, tomato paste, Worcestershire sauce, thyme, rosemary, and broth. Simmer for 10 minutes, or until the carrots are tender and the mixture is slightly thickened. Season with salt and pepper to taste.
3. **Assemble the Pie:**
    - Preheat your oven to 375°F (190°C).
    - Transfer the meat mixture to a baking dish (about 9x9 inches or similar size).
    - Spread the mashed potatoes evenly over the top of the meat mixture. Use a fork to create a pattern or texture on the surface of the mashed potatoes if desired.
4. **Bake:**

        - Bake in the preheated oven for 25-30 minutes, or until the top is golden brown and the filling is bubbling.
5. **Cool and Serve:**
        - Let the Shepherd's Pie cool for a few minutes before serving.

Enjoy your hearty and comforting rustic Shepherd's Pie!

**Spinach and Feta Stuffed Chicken**

**Ingredients:**

- 4 boneless, skinless chicken breasts
- 1 cup fresh spinach, chopped
- 1/2 cup feta cheese, crumbled
- 1/4 cup cream cheese, softened
- 2 cloves garlic, minced
- 1/4 cup grated Parmesan cheese
- 1/4 tsp dried oregano
- 1/4 tsp dried basil
- Salt and pepper to taste
- 1 tbsp olive oil
- 1/2 cup chicken broth

**Instructions:**

1. **Prepare the Filling:**
    - In a medium bowl, combine the chopped spinach, crumbled feta cheese, cream cheese, minced garlic, Parmesan cheese, oregano, basil, salt, and pepper. Mix until well combined.
2. **Prepare the Chicken:**
    - Preheat your oven to 375°F (190°C).
    - Using a sharp knife, carefully cut a pocket into each chicken breast by slicing horizontally, being careful not to cut all the way through.
3. **Stuff the Chicken:**
    - Spoon the spinach and feta mixture into each chicken breast pocket, dividing the filling evenly among the chicken breasts.
    - Secure the openings with toothpicks if necessary to hold the filling inside.
4. **Sear the Chicken:**
    - In an oven-safe skillet, heat the olive oil over medium-high heat.
    - Add the stuffed chicken breasts and sear for 2-3 minutes on each side, or until golden brown.
5. **Bake:**
    - Once seared, pour the chicken broth into the skillet around the chicken breasts.
    - Transfer the skillet to the preheated oven and bake for 20-25 minutes, or until the chicken is cooked through and the internal temperature reaches 165°F (74°C).
6. **Serve:**
    - Remove the chicken from the oven and let it rest for a few minutes before serving.
    - Discard the toothpicks and serve the chicken breasts with the pan juices drizzled over the top.

Enjoy your flavorful and juicy spinach and feta stuffed chicken!

**Sweet Potato and Black Bean Chili**

**Ingredients:**

- 2 tbsp olive oil
- 1 large onion, diced
- 2 cloves garlic, minced
- 1 large red bell pepper, diced
- 2 medium sweet potatoes, peeled and diced
- 1 can (14.5 oz) diced tomatoes
- 1 can (15 oz) black beans, drained and rinsed
- 1 cup vegetable or chicken broth
- 1 tbsp chili powder
- 1 tsp ground cumin
- 1/2 tsp smoked paprika
- 1/2 tsp dried oregano
- 1/4 tsp cayenne pepper (optional, for heat)
- Salt and pepper to taste
- 1 cup corn kernels (fresh, frozen, or canned)
- 1 lime, juiced
- Fresh cilantro, chopped (for garnish)
- Avocado slices (for garnish)
- Shredded cheese (optional, for garnish)

**Instructions:**

1. **Sauté Vegetables:**
    - Heat the olive oil in a large pot or Dutch oven over medium heat.
    - Add the diced onion and cook until softened, about 5 minutes.
    - Stir in the minced garlic and cook for another 1 minute.
2. **Add Vegetables:**
    - Add the red bell pepper and diced sweet potatoes to the pot. Cook for 5 minutes, stirring occasionally.
3. **Combine Ingredients:**
    - Stir in the diced tomatoes, black beans, vegetable or chicken broth, chili powder, cumin, smoked paprika, oregano, cayenne pepper (if using), salt, and pepper.
    - Bring the mixture to a boil, then reduce the heat to low. Simmer for 20-25 minutes, or until the sweet potatoes are tender and the chili has thickened.
4. **Add Corn and Finish:**
    - Stir in the corn kernels and cook for an additional 5 minutes, or until heated through.
    - Remove from heat and stir in the lime juice.
5. **Serve:**
    - Ladle the chili into bowls and garnish with chopped cilantro, avocado slices, and shredded cheese if desired.

Enjoy your hearty and nutritious sweet potato and black bean chili!

## Classic Beef Stroganoff

### Ingredients:

- 1 lb beef sirloin or tenderloin, thinly sliced into strips
- 2 tbsp olive oil or butter
- 1 medium onion, chopped
- 2 cloves garlic, minced
- 1 cup mushrooms, sliced (cremini or white)
- 1/4 cup all-purpose flour
- 1 cup beef broth
- 1 cup sour cream
- 1 tbsp Dijon mustard
- 1 tbsp Worcestershire sauce
- 1/2 tsp paprika
- Salt and pepper to taste
- Fresh parsley, chopped (for garnish)
- Cooked egg noodles or rice (for serving)

### Instructions:

1. **Prepare Beef:**
   - Heat the olive oil or butter in a large skillet over medium-high heat.
   - Add the sliced beef and cook until browned on all sides, about 2-3 minutes per side. Remove the beef from the skillet and set aside.
2. **Cook Vegetables:**
   - In the same skillet, add a bit more oil if needed. Sauté the chopped onion until softened, about 5 minutes.
   - Add the minced garlic and sliced mushrooms. Cook until the mushrooms are tender and browned, about 5 minutes.
3. **Make the Sauce:**
   - Sprinkle the flour over the vegetables and stir to combine. Cook for 1-2 minutes to remove the raw flour taste.
   - Gradually whisk in the beef broth, ensuring there are no lumps. Bring to a simmer and cook until the sauce has thickened, about 5 minutes.
4. **Add Beef and Finish:**
   - Return the cooked beef to the skillet along with any accumulated juices.
   - Stir in the sour cream, Dijon mustard, Worcestershire sauce, paprika, salt, and pepper. Cook until the beef is heated through and the sauce is creamy and well combined, about 3-5 minutes. Adjust seasoning if needed.
5. **Serve:**
   - Serve the beef stroganoff over cooked egg noodles or rice. Garnish with chopped fresh parsley.

Enjoy your classic and creamy beef stroganoff!

**Blueberry Lemon Muffins**

**Ingredients:**

- **For the Muffins:**
    - 1 1/2 cups all-purpose flour
    - 1/2 cup granulated sugar
    - 1/2 tsp baking soda
    - 1 1/2 tsp baking powder
    - 1/4 tsp salt
    - 1/2 cup unsalted butter, melted
    - 1/2 cup milk (whole or 2%)
    - 2 large eggs
    - 1 tsp vanilla extract
    - 1 tbsp lemon zest (from about 1 lemon)
    - 1 cup fresh or frozen blueberries (do not thaw if using frozen)
- **For the Lemon Glaze (optional):**
    - 1/2 cup powdered sugar
    - 2 tbsp lemon juice (from about 1 lemon)

**Instructions:**

1. **Preheat Oven:**
    - Preheat your oven to 375°F (190°C). Line a 12-cup muffin tin with paper liners or lightly grease it.
2. **Prepare Dry Ingredients:**
    - In a large bowl, whisk together the flour, granulated sugar, baking soda, baking powder, and salt.
3. **Mix Wet Ingredients:**
    - In another bowl, whisk together the melted butter, milk, eggs, vanilla extract, and lemon zest.
4. **Combine Ingredients:**
    - Pour the wet ingredients into the dry ingredients and stir until just combined. The batter will be thick.
    - Gently fold in the blueberries, being careful not to overmix to avoid breaking the berries.
5. **Fill Muffin Tin:**
    - Divide the batter evenly among the muffin cups, filling each about 2/3 full.
6. **Bake:**
    - Bake in the preheated oven for 20-25 minutes, or until a toothpick inserted into the center of a muffin comes out clean.
7. **Cool:**
    - Allow the muffins to cool in the tin for 5 minutes, then transfer them to a wire rack to cool completely.
8. **Make Glaze (Optional):**

- While the muffins cool, prepare the lemon glaze by whisking together the powdered sugar and lemon juice in a small bowl until smooth.
- Drizzle the glaze over the cooled muffins.

Enjoy your delicious blueberry lemon muffins with a burst of fresh flavor!

**Creamy Tomato Basil Soup**

**Ingredients:**

- 2 tbsp olive oil
- 1 medium onion, diced
- 2 cloves garlic, minced
- 1 can (28 oz) crushed tomatoes
- 2 cups vegetable or chicken broth
- 1 cup heavy cream
- 1 tbsp tomato paste
- 1 tsp dried basil (or 1 tbsp fresh basil, chopped)
- 1/2 tsp dried oregano
- 1/4 tsp sugar (optional, to taste)
- Salt and pepper to taste
- Fresh basil leaves (for garnish)
- Grated Parmesan cheese (for garnish, optional)

**Instructions:**

1. **Sauté Vegetables:**
   - Heat the olive oil in a large pot over medium heat. Add the diced onion and cook until softened, about 5 minutes.
   - Stir in the minced garlic and cook for another 1 minute, until fragrant.
2. **Add Tomatoes and Broth:**
   - Add the crushed tomatoes, vegetable or chicken broth, tomato paste, dried basil (or fresh basil), dried oregano, and sugar (if using). Stir to combine.
3. **Simmer:**
   - Bring the mixture to a simmer. Reduce heat to low and cook for 20 minutes, allowing the flavors to meld together.
4. **Blend Soup:**
   - Use an immersion blender to puree the soup until smooth. Alternatively, carefully transfer the soup in batches to a countertop blender and blend until smooth. (Be cautious with hot liquids.)
5. **Add Cream:**
   - Return the blended soup to the pot (if using a countertop blender). Stir in the heavy cream and heat through over low heat, about 5 minutes.
6. **Season:**
   - Taste and adjust seasoning with salt and pepper as needed.
7. **Serve:**
   - Ladle the soup into bowls and garnish with fresh basil leaves and grated Parmesan cheese if desired.

Enjoy your rich and comforting creamy tomato basil soup!

**Maple Pecan Carrots**

**Ingredients:**

- 1 lb carrots, peeled and sliced into 1/4-inch rounds
- 2 tbsp unsalted butter
- 2 tbsp pure maple syrup
- 1/4 cup chopped pecans
- 1/2 tsp ground cinnamon
- Salt and pepper to taste
- Fresh parsley, chopped (for garnish, optional)

**Instructions:**

1. **Cook Carrots:**
    - Bring a large pot of salted water to a boil. Add the sliced carrots and cook until tender, about 5-7 minutes.
    - Drain the carrots and set aside.
2. **Sauté Carrots:**
    - In a large skillet, melt the butter over medium heat.
    - Add the cooked carrots and sauté for 2-3 minutes, stirring to coat with the butter.
3. **Add Flavorings:**
    - Stir in the maple syrup, chopped pecans, and ground cinnamon. Cook for an additional 3-4 minutes, or until the carrots are well coated and the syrup has thickened slightly.
4. **Season and Serve:**
    - Season with salt and pepper to taste.
    - Garnish with chopped fresh parsley if desired.

Serve the maple pecan carrots warm as a delightful side dish!

# Roasted Brussels Sprouts with Bacon

## Ingredients:

- 1 1/2 lbs Brussels sprouts, trimmed and halved
- 4 slices bacon, diced
- 2 tbsp olive oil
- 1/2 tsp garlic powder
- 1/2 tsp onion powder
- Salt and pepper to taste
- 2 tbsp balsamic vinegar (optional, for extra flavor)
- Fresh parsley, chopped (for garnish, optional)

## Instructions:

1. **Preheat Oven:**
   - Preheat your oven to 400°F (200°C).
2. **Prepare Brussels Sprouts:**
   - In a large bowl, toss the halved Brussels sprouts with olive oil, garlic powder, onion powder, salt, and pepper.
3. **Add Bacon:**
   - Add the diced bacon to the bowl and toss to combine.
4. **Roast:**
   - Spread the Brussels sprouts and bacon in a single layer on a baking sheet.
   - Roast in the preheated oven for 20-25 minutes, or until the Brussels sprouts are tender and caramelized, and the bacon is crispy. Stir halfway through cooking for even roasting.
5. **Finish and Serve:**
   - If using, drizzle with balsamic vinegar and toss to coat.
   - Garnish with chopped fresh parsley if desired.

Serve the roasted Brussels sprouts with bacon as a savory and flavorful side dish!

**Beef and Barley Soup**

**Ingredients:**

- 1 lb beef stew meat, cut into cubes
- 2 tbsp olive oil
- 1 large onion, chopped
- 2 cloves garlic, minced
- 3 large carrots, diced
- 2 celery stalks, diced
- 1 cup barley (pearl or hulled)
- 1 can (14.5 oz) diced tomatoes
- 6 cups beef broth
- 1 cup water (or more if needed)
- 1 tsp dried thyme
- 1 tsp dried rosemary
- 1 bay leaf
- 1/2 cup frozen peas (optional)
- Salt and pepper to taste
- Fresh parsley, chopped (for garnish, optional)

**Instructions:**

1. **Brown the Beef:**
    - Heat olive oil in a large pot or Dutch oven over medium-high heat.
    - Add the beef cubes and cook until browned on all sides. Remove the beef from the pot and set aside.
2. **Sauté Vegetables:**
    - In the same pot, add the chopped onion, carrots, and celery. Cook until the vegetables are softened, about 5 minutes.
    - Stir in the minced garlic and cook for another 1 minute.
3. **Combine Ingredients:**
    - Return the browned beef to the pot.
    - Add the barley, diced tomatoes, beef broth, and water. Stir to combine.
    - Add the dried thyme, rosemary, and bay leaf. Season with salt and pepper to taste.
4. **Simmer:**
    - Bring the soup to a boil, then reduce the heat to low. Cover and simmer for 45-60 minutes, or until the beef is tender and the barley is cooked. Add more water if necessary to reach your desired consistency.
5. **Finish and Serve:**
    - If using, stir in the frozen peas during the last 5 minutes of cooking.
    - Remove the bay leaf and adjust seasoning with salt and pepper if needed.
    - Garnish with chopped fresh parsley if desired.

Serve the beef and barley soup hot, and enjoy this hearty and comforting meal!

## Raspberry Almond Cake

**Ingredients:**

- **For the Cake:**
    - 1 cup unsalted butter, softened
    - 1 cup granulated sugar
    - 4 large eggs
    - 1 tsp vanilla extract
    - 1 1/2 cups all-purpose flour
    - 1 cup almond flour (or finely ground almonds)
    - 1 1/2 tsp baking powder
    - 1/4 tsp salt
    - 1/2 cup milk
    - 1 cup fresh or frozen raspberries (do not thaw if using frozen)
- **For the Almond Glaze (optional):**
    - 1/2 cup powdered sugar
    - 2 tbsp milk
    - 1/2 tsp almond extract
- **For Garnish (optional):**
    - Sliced almonds
    - Fresh raspberries

**Instructions:**

1. **Preheat Oven:**
    - Preheat your oven to 350°F (175°C). Grease and flour a 9-inch round cake pan, or line it with parchment paper.
2. **Prepare Cake Batter:**
    - In a large bowl, cream together the softened butter and granulated sugar until light and fluffy.
    - Beat in the eggs one at a time, ensuring each egg is fully incorporated before adding the next.
    - Mix in the vanilla extract.
3. **Combine Dry Ingredients:**
    - In a separate bowl, whisk together the all-purpose flour, almond flour, baking powder, and salt.
4. **Combine Wet and Dry Ingredients:**
    - Gradually add the dry ingredients to the butter mixture, alternating with the milk. Begin and end with the dry ingredients. Mix until just combined.
    - Gently fold in the raspberries, being careful not to break them up too much.
5. **Bake:**
    - Pour the batter into the prepared cake pan and smooth the top.
    - Bake in the preheated oven for 35-40 minutes, or until a toothpick inserted into the center comes out clean and the cake is golden brown.

6. **Cool:**
    - Allow the cake to cool in the pan for 10 minutes, then transfer it to a wire rack to cool completely.
7. **Prepare Almond Glaze (Optional):**
    - In a small bowl, whisk together the powdered sugar, milk, and almond extract until smooth. Drizzle over the cooled cake.
8. **Garnish and Serve:**
    - Garnish with sliced almonds and fresh raspberries if desired.

Enjoy your delicious raspberry almond cake, perfect for a special occasion or a delightful treat!

# Garlic Parmesan Roasted Potatoes

## Ingredients:

- 1 1/2 lbs baby potatoes or small red potatoes, halved or quartered
- 3 tbsp olive oil
- 4 cloves garlic, minced
- 1/2 cup grated Parmesan cheese
- 1 tsp dried oregano
- 1/2 tsp dried thyme
- 1/4 tsp paprika
- Salt and pepper to taste
- Fresh parsley, chopped (for garnish, optional)

## Instructions:

1. **Preheat Oven:**
   - Preheat your oven to 400°F (200°C). Line a baking sheet with parchment paper or lightly grease it.
2. **Prepare Potatoes:**
   - In a large bowl, combine the halved or quartered potatoes with olive oil, minced garlic, Parmesan cheese, dried oregano, dried thyme, paprika, salt, and pepper. Toss until the potatoes are evenly coated.
3. **Roast Potatoes:**
   - Spread the potatoes in a single layer on the prepared baking sheet.
   - Roast in the preheated oven for 25-30 minutes, or until the potatoes are golden brown and crispy on the edges. Toss the potatoes halfway through cooking for even roasting.
4. **Garnish and Serve:**
   - Once roasted, remove from the oven and let cool slightly.
   - Garnish with chopped fresh parsley if desired.

Serve the garlic Parmesan roasted potatoes as a flavorful side dish with your favorite main course!

# Chicken and Mushroom Casserole

**Ingredients:**

- **For the Casserole:**
    - 1 lb boneless, skinless chicken breasts or thighs, cubed
    - 2 tbsp olive oil
    - 1 medium onion, chopped
    - 2 cloves garlic, minced
    - 8 oz mushrooms, sliced
    - 1 cup frozen peas (optional)
    - 1 can (10.5 oz) cream of chicken soup
    - 1 cup chicken broth
    - 1 cup sour cream or Greek yogurt
    - 1 tsp dried thyme
    - 1 tsp dried rosemary
    - Salt and pepper to taste
    - 1 cup shredded cheddar cheese (optional, for topping)
- **For the Topping (optional):**
    - 1 cup crushed crackers (such as Ritz or buttery crackers)
    - 2 tbsp melted butter

**Instructions:**

1. **Preheat Oven:**
    - Preheat your oven to 375°F (190°C). Grease a 9x13-inch baking dish or a similar-sized casserole dish.
2. **Cook Chicken:**
    - In a large skillet, heat the olive oil over medium heat.
    - Add the cubed chicken and cook until browned and cooked through, about 5-7 minutes. Remove from the skillet and set aside.
3. **Sauté Vegetables:**
    - In the same skillet, add the chopped onion and cook until softened, about 3 minutes.
    - Add the minced garlic and cook for another minute.
    - Stir in the sliced mushrooms and cook until they release their moisture and become tender, about 5 minutes.
4. **Combine Ingredients:**
    - Return the cooked chicken to the skillet with the onions and mushrooms.
    - Add the cream of chicken soup, chicken broth, sour cream (or Greek yogurt), dried thyme, dried rosemary, salt, and pepper. Stir to combine and heat through.
5. **Assemble Casserole:**
    - Pour the chicken and mushroom mixture into the prepared baking dish.
    - If using, sprinkle shredded cheddar cheese over the top.
6. **Prepare Topping (Optional):**

- In a small bowl, mix the crushed crackers with melted butter.
- Sprinkle the cracker mixture evenly over the casserole.
7. **Bake:**
    - Bake in the preheated oven for 25-30 minutes, or until the casserole is bubbly and the topping is golden brown.
8. **Cool and Serve:**
    - Let the casserole cool for a few minutes before serving.

Enjoy your hearty and comforting chicken and mushroom casserole!

**Pumpkin Spice Bread**

**Ingredients:**

- 1 1/2 cups all-purpose flour
- 1 cup granulated sugar
- 1/2 tsp baking powder
- 1/2 tsp baking soda
- 1/2 tsp salt
- 1 tsp ground cinnamon
- 1/2 tsp ground nutmeg
- 1/2 tsp ground ginger
- 1/4 tsp ground cloves
- 1/2 cup vegetable oil or melted butter
- 1 cup canned pumpkin puree (not pumpkin pie filling)
- 2 large eggs
- 1/4 cup water or milk
- 1 tsp vanilla extract
- 1/2 cup chopped nuts or chocolate chips (optional)

**Instructions:**

1. **Preheat Oven:**
    - Preheat your oven to 350°F (175°C). Grease and flour a 9x5-inch loaf pan or line it with parchment paper.
2. **Combine Dry Ingredients:**
    - In a medium bowl, whisk together the flour, sugar, baking powder, baking soda, salt, cinnamon, nutmeg, ginger, and cloves.
3. **Mix Wet Ingredients:**
    - In a large bowl, whisk together the oil (or melted butter), pumpkin puree, eggs, water (or milk), and vanilla extract until well combined.
4. **Combine Wet and Dry Ingredients:**
    - Gradually add the dry ingredients to the wet ingredients, stirring just until combined. If using, fold in the chopped nuts or chocolate chips.
5. **Pour and Bake:**
    - Pour the batter into the prepared loaf pan and smooth the top.
    - Bake in the preheated oven for 60-70 minutes, or until a toothpick inserted into the center comes out clean.
6. **Cool:**
    - Allow the bread to cool in the pan for 10 minutes, then transfer it to a wire rack to cool completely.

Serve the pumpkin spice bread warm or at room temperature. Enjoy its deliciously spiced flavor!

## Buttermilk Biscuits

**Ingredients:**

- 2 cups all-purpose flour
- 1 tbsp baking powder
- 1/2 tsp baking soda
- 1/2 tsp salt
- 1/2 cup cold unsalted butter, cut into small cubes
- 1 cup cold buttermilk

**Instructions:**

1. **Preheat Oven:**
   - Preheat your oven to 450°F (230°C). Lightly grease a baking sheet or line it with parchment paper.
2. **Mix Dry Ingredients:**
   - In a large bowl, whisk together the flour, baking powder, baking soda, and salt.
3. **Cut in Butter:**
   - Add the cold butter cubes to the flour mixture. Using a pastry cutter, two forks, or your fingers, work the butter into the flour until the mixture resembles coarse crumbs with pea-sized pieces of butter.
4. **Add Buttermilk:**
   - Pour the cold buttermilk into the flour mixture. Stir until just combined and the dough begins to come together. The dough will be somewhat sticky.
5. **Roll and Cut:**
   - Turn the dough out onto a lightly floured surface. Gently knead the dough 2-3 times to bring it together.
   - Roll the dough to about 1/2-inch thickness. Use a biscuit cutter or a glass to cut out biscuits. Place them close together on the prepared baking sheet for soft sides or spaced apart for crispier sides.
6. **Bake:**
   - Bake in the preheated oven for 10-12 minutes, or until the biscuits are golden brown on top.
7. **Cool and Serve:**
   - Allow the biscuits to cool slightly on a wire rack before serving.

Enjoy your homemade buttermilk biscuits warm, with butter, honey, or your favorite spread!

**Roasted Vegetable Medley**

**Ingredients:**

- 3 cups of mixed vegetables (such as bell peppers, carrots, zucchini, red onions, and potatoes), cut into bite-sized pieces
- 3 tbsp olive oil
- 1 tsp dried thyme
- 1 tsp dried rosemary
- 1/2 tsp garlic powder
- 1/2 tsp onion powder
- 1/2 tsp paprika
- Salt and pepper to taste
- Fresh parsley, chopped (for garnish, optional)

**Instructions:**

1. **Preheat Oven:**
   - Preheat your oven to 425°F (220°C). Line a baking sheet with parchment paper or lightly grease it.
2. **Prepare Vegetables:**
   - In a large bowl, combine the mixed vegetables.
3. **Season Vegetables:**
   - Drizzle the olive oil over the vegetables and toss to coat evenly.
   - Sprinkle the dried thyme, dried rosemary, garlic powder, onion powder, paprika, salt, and pepper over the vegetables. Toss again until all the vegetables are evenly coated with the seasonings.
4. **Roast Vegetables:**
   - Spread the seasoned vegetables in a single layer on the prepared baking sheet.
   - Roast in the preheated oven for 25-30 minutes, or until the vegetables are tender and lightly browned. Stir the vegetables halfway through the cooking time for even roasting.
5. **Garnish and Serve:**
   - Once roasted, remove from the oven and let cool slightly.
   - Garnish with chopped fresh parsley if desired.

Serve the roasted vegetable medley as a flavorful and healthy side dish with your favorite main course!

**Cranberry Walnut Salad**

**Ingredients:**

- **For the Salad:**
    - 6 cups mixed salad greens (such as spinach, arugula, and baby greens)
    - 1/2 cup dried cranberries
    - 1/2 cup toasted walnuts
    - 1/2 cup crumbled feta cheese or goat cheese (optional)
    - 1/2 red onion, thinly sliced (optional)
    - 1 apple or pear, thinly sliced (optional)
- **For the Dressing:**
    - 1/4 cup extra-virgin olive oil
    - 2 tbsp balsamic vinegar
    - 1 tbsp honey or maple syrup
    - 1 tsp Dijon mustard
    - Salt and pepper to taste

**Instructions:**

1. **Prepare the Salad:**
    - In a large salad bowl, combine the mixed greens, dried cranberries, toasted walnuts, and crumbled cheese (if using).
    - If desired, add thinly sliced red onion and apple or pear slices for extra flavor and crunch.
2. **Make the Dressing:**
    - In a small bowl or jar, whisk together the olive oil, balsamic vinegar, honey (or maple syrup), Dijon mustard, salt, and pepper until well combined.
3. **Assemble and Toss:**
    - Drizzle the dressing over the salad and toss gently to coat the ingredients evenly.
4. **Serve:**
    - Serve the salad immediately, or chill in the refrigerator for up to 30 minutes before serving.

Enjoy your refreshing and flavorful cranberry walnut salad as a light lunch or a delightful side dish!

# Creamy Broccoli Cheddar Soup

**Ingredients:**

- 2 tbsp unsalted butter
- 1 medium onion, chopped
- 2 cloves garlic, minced
- 4 cups broccoli florets (fresh or frozen)
- 3 cups chicken or vegetable broth
- 1 cup milk (whole or 2%)
- 1 cup heavy cream
- 2 cups shredded sharp cheddar cheese
- 1/2 tsp dried thyme (optional)
- Salt and pepper to taste
- 1/4 cup all-purpose flour (for thickening, optional)
- 1/2 cup grated Parmesan cheese (optional, for extra flavor)

**Instructions:**

1. **Sauté Aromatics:**
   - In a large pot, melt the butter over medium heat.
   - Add the chopped onion and cook until softened and translucent, about 5 minutes.
   - Stir in the minced garlic and cook for an additional minute.
2. **Cook Broccoli:**
   - Add the broccoli florets to the pot and stir to combine.
   - Pour in the chicken or vegetable broth and bring to a boil.
   - Reduce heat and simmer until the broccoli is tender, about 10-15 minutes.
3. **Blend Soup:**
   - Using an immersion blender, puree the soup until smooth. Alternatively, you can carefully transfer the soup in batches to a blender and blend until smooth, then return to the pot.
4. **Add Cream and Cheese:**
   - Stir in the milk and heavy cream, and heat through without boiling.
   - Gradually add the shredded cheddar cheese, stirring until melted and fully incorporated. If using, add the grated Parmesan cheese as well.
5. **Thicken Soup (Optional):**
   - If you prefer a thicker soup, whisk together the flour with a little water to make a slurry. Stir the slurry into the soup and cook for a few more minutes until the soup thickens.
6. **Season and Serve:**
   - Season the soup with dried thyme (if using), salt, and pepper to taste.
   - Serve hot, garnished with additional shredded cheddar cheese or fresh herbs if desired.

Enjoy your creamy broccoli cheddar soup with crusty bread or a side salad!

**Herb-Infused Roast Beef**

**Ingredients:**

- 3-4 lb beef roast (such as ribeye, sirloin, or chuck)
- 2 tbsp olive oil
- 4 cloves garlic, minced
- 2 tbsp fresh rosemary, finely chopped (or 2 tsp dried rosemary)
- 2 tbsp fresh thyme, finely chopped (or 2 tsp dried thyme)
- 1 tbsp fresh parsley, finely chopped (or 1 tsp dried parsley)
- 1 tbsp Dijon mustard
- 1 tbsp Worcestershire sauce
- Salt and black pepper to taste
- 1 cup beef broth
- 1/2 cup red wine (optional)

**Instructions:**

1. **Preheat Oven:**
    - Preheat your oven to 375°F (190°C).
2. **Prepare Herb Rub:**
    - In a small bowl, mix together the minced garlic, rosemary, thyme, parsley, Dijon mustard, Worcestershire sauce, olive oil, salt, and pepper.
3. **Season the Roast:**
    - Rub the herb mixture all over the beef roast, making sure to cover it evenly.
4. **Sear the Roast:**
    - Heat a large ovenproof skillet or roasting pan over medium-high heat. Add a little olive oil if needed.
    - Sear the beef roast on all sides until browned, about 3-4 minutes per side.
5. **Roast Beef:**
    - Once seared, transfer the skillet or roasting pan to the preheated oven.
    - Roast for about 20 minutes per pound for medium-rare, or until a meat thermometer inserted into the center of the roast reads 135°F (57°C) for medium-rare. Adjust cooking time based on your preferred level of doneness.
6. **Prepare the Pan Sauce (Optional):**
    - While the roast is resting, place the skillet or roasting pan over medium heat on the stove.
    - Add beef broth and red wine (if using) to the pan, scraping up any browned bits from the bottom.
    - Simmer the mixture until reduced by half, then strain if desired.
7. **Rest and Serve:**
    - Remove the roast from the oven and let it rest for 10-15 minutes before slicing.
    - Serve with the pan sauce drizzled over the top or on the side.

Enjoy your herb-infused roast beef with your favorite sides and accompaniments!

# Pumpkin Risotto

## Ingredients:

- 4 cups chicken or vegetable broth
- 1 cup canned pumpkin puree (not pumpkin pie filling)
- 2 tbsp olive oil
- 1 small onion, finely chopped
- 2 cloves garlic, minced
- 1 1/2 cups Arborio rice
- 1/2 cup dry white wine (optional)
- 1/2 cup grated Parmesan cheese
- 2 tbsp unsalted butter
- 1/2 tsp dried sage or 1 tsp fresh sage, chopped
- Salt and black pepper to taste
- Fresh parsley or additional sage for garnish (optional)

## Instructions:

1. **Heat Broth:**
   - In a saucepan, heat the broth over low heat to keep it warm. Stir in the pumpkin puree and set aside.
2. **Sauté Aromatics:**
   - In a large skillet or saucepan, heat the olive oil over medium heat.
   - Add the chopped onion and cook until softened and translucent, about 5 minutes.
   - Stir in the minced garlic and cook for another minute.
3. **Cook Rice:**
   - Add the Arborio rice to the skillet and stir to coat with the oil and aromatics. Cook for 1-2 minutes, until the rice starts to turn slightly translucent around the edges.
4. **Deglaze with Wine (Optional):**
   - Pour in the white wine, if using, and cook, stirring constantly, until the wine has mostly evaporated.
5. **Add Broth:**
   - Begin adding the warm broth mixture, one ladleful at a time, to the rice. Stir frequently and let the rice absorb the liquid before adding more.
   - Continue this process until the rice is creamy and cooked al dente, about 18-20 minutes. You may not need all the broth.
6. **Finish Risotto:**
   - Stir in the grated Parmesan cheese and butter until melted and combined.
   - Add the dried sage or fresh sage, and season with salt and black pepper to taste.
7. **Serve:**
   - Spoon the risotto onto plates or into bowls.
   - Garnish with fresh parsley or additional sage if desired.

Enjoy your creamy and comforting pumpkin risotto as a delightful side dish or a satisfying main course!

# Spaghetti Squash with Marinara Sauce

## Ingredients

**For the Spaghetti Squash:**

- 1 medium spaghetti squash
- 1-2 tablespoons olive oil
- Salt and pepper, to taste

**For the Marinara Sauce:**

- 1 tablespoon olive oil
- 1 small onion, finely chopped
- 2-3 cloves garlic, minced
- 1 can (15 oz) crushed tomatoes
- 1 tablespoon tomato paste
- 1 teaspoon dried basil
- 1 teaspoon dried oregano
- 1/2 teaspoon sugar (optional, to balance acidity)
- Salt and pepper, to taste
- Fresh basil or parsley, for garnish (optional)

## Instructions

**Preparing the Spaghetti Squash:**

1. **Preheat Oven:** Preheat your oven to 400°F (200°C).
2. **Prepare Squash:** Cut the spaghetti squash in half lengthwise. Scoop out the seeds with a spoon.
3. **Season and Roast:** Brush the cut sides with olive oil and season with salt and pepper. Place the squash cut-side down on a baking sheet lined with parchment paper.
4. **Bake:** Roast for 40-45 minutes, or until the squash is tender and the flesh easily shreds into spaghetti-like strands with a fork.
5. **Shred:** Let the squash cool slightly, then use a fork to scrape out the strands. Set aside.

**Making the Marinara Sauce:**

1. **Cook Onion and Garlic:** Heat olive oil in a saucepan over medium heat. Add the chopped onion and cook until soft and translucent, about 5 minutes. Add the minced garlic and cook for another 1-2 minutes until fragrant.
2. **Add Tomatoes and Seasonings:** Stir in the crushed tomatoes, tomato paste, dried basil, dried oregano, and sugar (if using). Season with salt and pepper to taste.
3. **Simmer:** Bring to a simmer, reduce the heat to low, and let it cook for about 15-20 minutes, stirring occasionally, until the sauce thickens and the flavors meld together.

4. **Adjust Seasoning:** Taste and adjust seasoning as needed.

**Assembling:**

1. **Combine:** Toss the spaghetti squash strands with the marinara sauce until well coated.
2. **Serve:** Divide the squash between plates and top with extra marinara sauce if desired. Garnish with fresh basil or parsley if you like.

Enjoy your delicious and healthy spaghetti squash with marinara sauce! If you want to add some protein, you can serve it with grilled chicken, meatballs, or a sprinkle of Parmesan cheese.

**Apple Harvest Salad**

## Ingredients

### For the Salad:

- 4 cups mixed salad greens (such as spinach, arugula, and baby kale)
- 2 apples, thinly sliced (such as Honeycrisp, Fuji, or Granny Smith)
- 1/2 cup crumbled feta cheese or goat cheese
- 1/4 cup toasted pecans or walnuts
- 1/4 cup dried cranberries or raisins
- 1/4 red onion, thinly sliced
- 1/2 cucumber, sliced (optional)

### For the Dressing:

- 3 tablespoons extra-virgin olive oil
- 2 tablespoons apple cider vinegar
- 1 tablespoon honey or maple syrup
- 1 teaspoon Dijon mustard
- Salt and pepper, to taste

## Instructions

### Prepare the Salad:

1. **Prepare the Apples:** Core and thinly slice the apples. If you want to prevent them from browning, toss them in a little lemon juice.
2. **Toast Nuts:** In a dry skillet over medium heat, toast the pecans or walnuts until fragrant and slightly browned, about 3-5 minutes. Stir frequently to prevent burning. Let them cool.
3. **Slice Vegetables:** Thinly slice the red onion and cucumber, if using.

### Make the Dressing:

1. **Combine Ingredients:** In a small bowl or jar, whisk together the olive oil, apple cider vinegar, honey or maple syrup, and Dijon mustard until well combined.
2. **Season:** Taste and season with salt and pepper to your liking.

### Assemble the Salad:

1. **Combine Ingredients:** In a large bowl, toss together the salad greens, apple slices, crumbled cheese, toasted nuts, dried cranberries or raisins, and red onion.
2. **Dress the Salad:** Drizzle the dressing over the salad and toss gently to coat all the ingredients evenly.
3. **Serve:** Serve immediately or refrigerate for up to an hour before serving. If making ahead, keep the dressing separate until ready to serve.

## Tips:

- **For Extra Flavor:** Add grilled chicken or roasted turkey for a protein boost.
- **For Added Crunch:** Consider adding some thinly sliced celery or shredded carrots.
- **For Freshness:** Use freshly made dressing rather than store-bought for the best flavor.

Enjoy your crisp, autumn-inspired Apple Harvest Salad!

**Cornbread Stuffing**

## Ingredients

### For the Cornbread:

- 1 batch of homemade cornbread (or about 4 cups of store-bought, crumbled)
- 1 cup buttermilk
- 1/4 cup melted butter
- 1 large egg

### For the Stuffing:

- 2 tablespoons butter
- 1 medium onion, finely chopped
- 2 celery stalks, chopped
- 2 cloves garlic, minced
- 1 cup chicken or vegetable broth
- 1 teaspoon dried sage
- 1 teaspoon dried thyme
- 1/2 teaspoon dried rosemary
- Salt and pepper, to taste
- 1/4 cup fresh parsley, chopped (optional)
- 1/2 cup dried cranberries or raisins (optional, for a touch of sweetness)

## Instructions

### Prepare the Cornbread:

1. **Make Cornbread:** If making cornbread from scratch, follow your preferred recipe. Allow it to cool completely, then crumble into small pieces. You should have about 4 cups of crumbled cornbread.

### Prepare the Stuffing:

1. **Preheat Oven:** Preheat your oven to 350°F (175°C).
2. **Cook Vegetables:** In a large skillet, melt the butter over medium heat. Add the chopped onion and celery. Cook until softened, about 5-7 minutes. Add the minced garlic and cook for another minute until fragrant.
3. **Combine Ingredients:** In a large mixing bowl, combine the crumbled cornbread with the cooked vegetables. Add the chicken or vegetable broth, dried sage, thyme, rosemary, salt, and pepper. Stir until everything is well mixed and the cornbread is slightly moist but not soggy. If using, fold in the fresh parsley and dried cranberries or raisins.
4. **Transfer to Baking Dish:** Transfer the stuffing mixture to a greased baking dish (about 9x13 inches). Smooth the top with a spatula.
5. **Bake:** Bake for 25-30 minutes, or until the top is golden brown and crispy.

## Tips:

- **Dry Cornbread:** For a more traditional stuffing texture, use day-old cornbread or let the crumbled cornbread sit out for a few hours to dry out slightly before using.
- **Additional Flavor:** You can add cooked sausage, bacon, or mushrooms for extra flavor.
- **Make Ahead:** You can prepare the stuffing a day in advance. Just store it covered in the refrigerator and bake it on the day of serving.

Enjoy your cornbread stuffing as a delicious side dish for your holiday meals or any time you want a comforting, savory treat!

**Chicken Marsala**

## Ingredients

- 4 boneless, skinless chicken breasts
- Salt and black pepper, to taste
- 1/2 cup all-purpose flour, for dredging
- 2 tablespoons olive oil
- 2 tablespoons unsalted butter
- 1 cup sliced mushrooms (such as cremini or button)
- 3/4 cup Marsala wine
- 3/4 cup chicken broth
- 1 tablespoon chopped fresh parsley (optional, for garnish)

## Instructions

1. **Prepare the Chicken:**
   - Place each chicken breast between two sheets of plastic wrap or parchment paper. Using a meat mallet or rolling pin, pound the chicken breasts to an even thickness (about 1/2 inch thick). This helps them cook evenly.
   - Season both sides of the chicken breasts with salt and black pepper. Dredge the chicken breasts in flour, shaking off any excess.
2. **Cook the Chicken:**
   - In a large skillet, heat the olive oil and 1 tablespoon of butter over medium-high heat.
   - Add the chicken breasts and cook for 4-5 minutes per side, or until golden brown and cooked through (internal temperature should reach 165°F or 74°C). Remove the chicken from the skillet and set aside on a plate.
3. **Make the Sauce:**
   - In the same skillet, add the remaining 1 tablespoon of butter. Add the sliced mushrooms and cook until they are browned and tender, about 5 minutes.
   - Pour in the Marsala wine and cook for 1-2 minutes, scraping up any browned bits from the bottom of the skillet with a wooden spoon.
   - Add the chicken broth and bring the mixture to a simmer. Cook for another 5 minutes, or until the sauce has reduced and thickened slightly.
4. **Combine and Serve:**
   - Return the cooked chicken breasts to the skillet, along with any juices that have accumulated on the plate. Simmer for 3-4 minutes, or until the chicken is heated through and coated with the sauce.
   - Garnish with chopped fresh parsley, if desired.
5. **Serve:**
   - Serve the Chicken Marsala over pasta, rice, or with a side of vegetables. The rich sauce is delicious with mashed potatoes as well.

## Tips:

- **Marsala Wine:** Marsala wine is a key ingredient, providing the distinctive flavor. If you can't find Marsala, a dry white wine or sherry can be used as a substitute, though the flavor will be different.
- **Mushrooms:** Feel free to use a mix of mushrooms for added depth of flavor.
- **Thickening Sauce:** If you prefer a thicker sauce, you can whisk in a slurry of cornstarch and water (1 tablespoon cornstarch mixed with 1 tablespoon water) to the simmering sauce.

Enjoy your Chicken Marsala with a nice glass of Marsala wine to complement the meal!

**Pecan-Crusted Salmon**

## Ingredients

- 4 salmon fillets (6 ounces each)
- Salt and black pepper, to taste
- 1/2 cup finely chopped pecans
- 1/4 cup panko breadcrumbs
- 1/4 cup grated Parmesan cheese (optional)
- 2 tablespoons Dijon mustard
- 2 tablespoons honey
- 2 tablespoons olive oil or melted butter
- 1 tablespoon fresh lemon juice (optional, for serving)
- Lemon wedges (optional, for serving)

## Instructions

1. **Preheat Oven:** Preheat your oven to 400°F (200°C). Line a baking sheet with parchment paper or lightly grease it.
2. **Prepare the Salmon:**
   - Pat the salmon fillets dry with paper towels. Season both sides with salt and black pepper.
   - In a small bowl, mix together the Dijon mustard and honey. Brush this mixture evenly over the top of each salmon fillet.
3. **Prepare the Pecan Crust:**
   - In a separate bowl, combine the finely chopped pecans, panko breadcrumbs, and grated Parmesan cheese (if using). Stir in the olive oil or melted butter until the mixture is well coated and resembles coarse crumbs.
4. **Coat the Salmon:**
   - Press the pecan mixture onto the mustard-coated side of each salmon fillet, pressing down gently to adhere.
5. **Bake the Salmon:**
   - Place the salmon fillets on the prepared baking sheet, crust-side up. Bake in the preheated oven for 12-15 minutes, or until the salmon is cooked through and flakes easily with a fork. The internal temperature should reach 145°F (63°C).
6. **Optional Finishing Touch:**
   - For added flavor, drizzle with fresh lemon juice right before serving. Serve with lemon wedges on the side.

## Tips:

- **Pecan Size:** Make sure the pecans are finely chopped so they form a nice crust. You can use a food processor to chop them if you prefer.
- **Crispier Crust:** For an extra crispy crust, you can briefly broil the salmon for the last 1-2 minutes of baking, keeping a close eye to prevent burning.

- **Serve With:** This dish pairs well with a variety of sides, such as roasted vegetables, quinoa, or a fresh green salad.

Enjoy your flavorful and crunchy pecan-crusted salmon!

**Maple-Glazed Carrots**

## Ingredients

- 1 pound baby carrots or sliced carrots (about 4 cups)
- 2 tablespoons unsalted butter
- 2 tablespoons pure maple syrup
- 1 tablespoon brown sugar (optional, for extra sweetness)
- 1/2 teaspoon ground cinnamon (optional, for added warmth)
- Salt and black pepper, to taste
- Fresh parsley or thyme, chopped (optional, for garnish)

## Instructions

1. **Prepare the Carrots:**
   - If using baby carrots, rinse them under cold water. If using regular carrots, peel them and cut them into bite-sized pieces or thin rounds.
2. **Cook the Carrots:**
   - Place the carrots in a medium saucepan and cover with water. Bring to a boil over medium-high heat. Reduce the heat and simmer for about 5-7 minutes, or until the carrots are tender but still crisp.
   - Drain the carrots and set aside.
3. **Make the Maple Glaze:**
   - In the same saucepan, melt the butter over medium heat. Add the maple syrup and brown sugar (if using). Stir until the brown sugar is dissolved and the mixture is smooth.
   - If you're using ground cinnamon, add it to the glaze and stir to combine.
4. **Glaze the Carrots:**
   - Return the cooked carrots to the saucepan with the maple glaze. Toss the carrots in the glaze and cook for 2-3 minutes, or until the carrots are evenly coated and heated through. Season with salt and black pepper to taste.
5. **Serve:**
   - Transfer the glazed carrots to a serving dish. Garnish with chopped fresh parsley or thyme if desired.

## Tips:

- **Consistency:** If the glaze is too thick, you can thin it out with a small amount of water or additional maple syrup.
- **Variations:** For a touch of spice, you can add a pinch of nutmeg or a splash of orange juice to the glaze.
- **Make Ahead:** You can prepare the carrots and glaze in advance and reheat them just before serving.

These maple-glazed carrots are a perfect side dish for holiday dinners, weeknight meals, or any time you want to add a sweet and savory touch to your plate. Enjoy!

**Beef and Vegetable Skewers**

## Ingredients

**For the Beef Marinade:**

- 1 pound sirloin steak or tenderloin, cut into 1-inch cubes
- 1/4 cup olive oil
- 1/4 cup soy sauce
- 2 tablespoons balsamic vinegar or red wine vinegar
- 2 tablespoons honey or brown sugar
- 2 cloves garlic, minced
- 1 teaspoon dried oregano
- 1 teaspoon dried thyme
- Salt and black pepper, to taste

**For the Vegetables:**

- 1 red bell pepper, cut into 1-inch pieces
- 1 yellow bell pepper, cut into 1-inch pieces
- 1 red onion, cut into wedges
- 1 zucchini, sliced into 1/2-inch rounds
- 8-10 cherry tomatoes

## Instructions

1. **Marinate the Beef:**
    - In a bowl, whisk together the olive oil, soy sauce, balsamic vinegar, honey, garlic, oregano, thyme, salt, and pepper.
    - Add the beef cubes to the marinade, tossing to coat. Cover and refrigerate for at least 30 minutes, or up to 4 hours for more flavor.
2. **Prepare the Vegetables:**
    - While the beef is marinating, prepare the vegetables. Cut the bell peppers, onion, and zucchini as described.
3. **Preheat the Grill or Broiler:**
    - Preheat your grill to medium-high heat, or set your broiler to high if cooking indoors.
4. **Assemble the Skewers:**
    - Thread the marinated beef and vegetables onto skewers, alternating between beef and vegetables. If you're using wooden skewers, soak them in water for 30 minutes beforehand to prevent burning.
5. **Cook the Skewers:**
    - **Grilling:** Place the skewers on the grill. Grill for 8-10 minutes, turning occasionally, until the beef is cooked to your desired level of doneness and the vegetables are tender and slightly charred.
    - **Broiling:** Place the skewers on a broiler pan and broil for 8-10 minutes, turning once halfway through, until the beef is cooked and the vegetables are tender.

6. **Serve:**
    - Remove the skewers from the grill or broiler and let them rest for a few minutes. Serve with your favorite dipping sauces or alongside rice, couscous, or a fresh salad.

## Tips:

- **Marinating Time:** For the best flavor, marinate the beef for several hours if possible. Even a 30-minute marinade will add good flavor.
- **Vegetable Variations:** Feel free to add other vegetables like mushrooms, squash, or asparagus. Just make sure to cut them into similar sizes to ensure even cooking.
- **Cooking Doneness:** For beef, aim for an internal temperature of 135°F (57°C) for medium-rare, 145°F (63°C) for medium, and 160°F (71°C) for well-done.

Enjoy your flavorful beef and vegetable skewers with your favorite sides!

**Garlic Butter Shrimp**

## Ingredients

- 1 pound large shrimp, peeled and deveined (tails on or off as preferred)
- 3 tablespoons unsalted butter
- 4 cloves garlic, minced
- 1/4 teaspoon red pepper flakes (optional, for a touch of heat)
- 1 tablespoon fresh lemon juice (about 1/2 lemon)
- 2 tablespoons chopped fresh parsley
- Salt and black pepper, to taste
- Lemon wedges, for serving

## Instructions

1. **Prepare the Shrimp:**
   - Pat the shrimp dry with paper towels. Season them lightly with salt and black pepper.
2. **Cook the Shrimp:**
   - In a large skillet, melt the butter over medium heat.
   - Add the minced garlic and red pepper flakes (if using). Cook for about 1 minute, stirring frequently, until the garlic is fragrant but not browned.
   - Add the shrimp to the skillet in a single layer. Cook for about 2-3 minutes on each side, or until the shrimp are pink and opaque. Be careful not to overcook them, as they can become tough.
3. **Add Lemon Juice and Parsley:**
   - Once the shrimp are cooked, squeeze the fresh lemon juice over them and toss in the chopped parsley. Stir to combine and coat the shrimp in the garlic butter sauce.
4. **Serve:**
   - Transfer the shrimp to a serving dish and drizzle with any remaining garlic butter from the skillet. Serve immediately with lemon wedges on the side.

## Tips:

- **Shrimp Size:** Large or jumbo shrimp work best for this recipe. If using smaller shrimp, adjust the cooking time accordingly.
- **Butter:** For a richer flavor, you can use more butter or add a splash of white wine to the sauce.
- **Extra Flavor:** Add a pinch of paprika or a splash of hot sauce for extra flavor and a bit of heat.

## Serving Suggestions:

- Serve garlic butter shrimp over pasta or rice to make a complete meal.
- Pair with a side of steamed vegetables or a fresh salad for a lighter option.

- Use the garlic butter sauce as a dipping sauce for crusty bread.

Enjoy your flavorful and easy-to-make garlic butter shrimp!

**Gingerbread Cookies**

## Ingredients

**For the Cookies:**

- 3 1/4 cups all-purpose flour
- 1/4 teaspoon baking soda
- 1/2 teaspoon baking powder
- 1 tablespoon ground ginger
- 1 tablespoon ground cinnamon
- 1/2 teaspoon ground cloves
- 1/4 teaspoon salt
- 1/2 cup unsalted butter, softened
- 1/2 cup granulated sugar
- 1/2 cup packed brown sugar
- 1 large egg
- 1/2 cup unsulfured molasses

**For the Royal Icing (optional):**

- 2 large egg whites
- 3 1/2 cups powdered sugar
- 1 teaspoon lemon juice or white vinegar

## Instructions

**Prepare the Cookies:**

1. **Preheat Oven:** Preheat your oven to 350°F (175°C). Line baking sheets with parchment paper.
2. **Mix Dry Ingredients:** In a medium bowl, whisk together the flour, baking soda, baking powder, ginger, cinnamon, cloves, and salt.
3. **Cream Butter and Sugars:** In a large bowl, use an electric mixer to beat the softened butter, granulated sugar, and brown sugar until light and fluffy.
4. **Add Egg and Molasses:** Beat in the egg until well combined. Mix in the molasses.
5. **Combine Ingredients:** Gradually add the dry ingredients to the butter mixture, mixing on low speed until the dough comes together.
6. **Chill the Dough:** Divide the dough into two portions, wrap each in plastic wrap, and refrigerate for at least 1 hour to firm up.
7. **Roll Out and Cut:** On a lightly floured surface, roll out one portion of the dough to about 1/4 inch thickness. Use cookie cutters to cut out shapes and transfer them to the prepared baking sheets.
8. **Bake:** Bake in the preheated oven for 8-10 minutes, or until the edges are firm but the centers are still soft. Allow the cookies to cool on the baking sheets for a few minutes before transferring to wire racks to cool completely.

**Prepare the Royal Icing (Optional):**

1. **Beat Egg Whites:** In a large bowl, beat the egg whites until frothy.
2. **Add Powdered Sugar:** Gradually add the powdered sugar and lemon juice (or vinegar), and continue to beat until stiff peaks form.
3. **Decorate:** Use the royal icing to decorate the cooled cookies. You can use a piping bag or a plastic sandwich bag with the tip cut off. Let the icing set before storing the cookies.

## Tips:

- **Consistency:** If the royal icing is too thick, add a few drops of water. If too thin, add more powdered sugar.
- **Decorating:** You can use colored sugars, sprinkles, or edible decorations to enhance your cookies.
- **Storage:** Store decorated or undecorated cookies in an airtight container at room temperature for up to 1 week. They also freeze well for up to 3 months.

Enjoy baking and decorating your gingerbread cookies! They're perfect for sharing with friends and family during the holiday season.

**Creamy Spinach Artichoke Dip**

## Ingredients

- 1 (10-ounce) package frozen chopped spinach, thawed and drained
- 1 (14-ounce) can artichoke hearts, drained and chopped
- 1 cup sour cream
- 1 cup mayonnaise
- 1 cup grated Parmesan cheese
- 1 cup shredded mozzarella cheese
- 3 cloves garlic, minced
- 1/2 teaspoon onion powder
- 1/2 teaspoon garlic powder
- Salt and black pepper, to taste
- Optional: 1/4 teaspoon crushed red pepper flakes (for a bit of heat)
- Fresh parsley, chopped (for garnish, optional)

## Instructions

1. **Preheat Oven:** Preheat your oven to 375°F (190°C).
2. **Prepare Ingredients:**
    - Thaw the frozen spinach and squeeze out as much moisture as possible using a clean kitchen towel or paper towels.
    - Drain and chop the artichoke hearts if they're not already chopped.
3. **Mix the Dip:**
    - In a large mixing bowl, combine the drained spinach, chopped artichokes, sour cream, mayonnaise, Parmesan cheese, mozzarella cheese, minced garlic, onion powder, garlic powder, salt, and black pepper. If using, add the crushed red pepper flakes.
4. **Transfer to Baking Dish:**
    - Spread the mixture evenly into a baking dish (a 9-inch pie dish or an 8x8-inch baking dish works well).
5. **Bake:**
    - Bake in the preheated oven for 25-30 minutes, or until the dip is hot and bubbly, and the top is golden brown.
6. **Garnish and Serve:**
    - Garnish with chopped fresh parsley if desired. Serve warm with tortilla chips, pita chips, sliced baguette, or fresh vegetables for dipping.

## Tips:

- **Make Ahead:** You can prepare the dip a day in advance. Assemble it and store it in the refrigerator, then bake it just before serving.
- **Texture:** If you prefer a smoother dip, you can blend the mixture before baking or use a food processor.
- **Creaminess:** For an even creamier dip, you can add a bit of cream cheese to the mixture.

Enjoy your creamy spinach artichoke dip! It's sure to be a hit at your next gathering.

**Chicken and Rice Soup**

**Ingredients**

- 1 tablespoon olive oil
- 1 medium onion, chopped
- 2 carrots, peeled and diced
- 2 celery stalks, diced
- 3 cloves garlic, minced
- 6 cups chicken broth
- 1 cup cooked chicken, shredded or diced (rotisserie chicken works well)
- 1 cup long-grain white rice or jasmine rice
- 1 bay leaf
- 1 teaspoon dried thyme
- 1/2 teaspoon dried rosemary
- Salt and black pepper, to taste
- 1 cup frozen peas (optional)
- 2 tablespoons chopped fresh parsley (optional, for garnish)
- Juice of 1 lemon (optional, for a touch of brightness)

## Instructions

1. **Sauté the Vegetables:**
    - In a large pot, heat the olive oil over medium heat. Add the chopped onion, carrots, and celery. Sauté for about 5-7 minutes, or until the vegetables are softened.
2. **Add Garlic:**
    - Add the minced garlic and cook for another 1 minute, stirring frequently.
3. **Add Broth and Seasonings:**
    - Pour in the chicken broth and add the bay leaf, dried thyme, dried rosemary, salt, and black pepper. Bring the mixture to a boil.
4. **Cook the Rice:**
    - Add the rice to the boiling broth. Reduce the heat to low, cover, and simmer for about 15-20 minutes, or until the rice is tender.
5. **Add Chicken and Peas:**
    - Stir in the cooked chicken and frozen peas (if using). Simmer for another 5 minutes, or until the chicken is heated through and the peas are tender.
6. **Finish the Soup:**
    - Remove the bay leaf. If desired, stir in the lemon juice for added brightness. Taste and adjust seasoning with more salt and pepper if needed.
7. **Serve:**
    - Ladle the soup into bowls and garnish with chopped fresh parsley if desired. Serve hot with crusty bread or crackers on the side.

## Tips:

- **Chicken:** Use leftover cooked chicken or rotisserie chicken for convenience. If cooking chicken specifically for the soup, you can poach chicken breasts or thighs in the broth until cooked through, then shred or dice.
- **Rice:** If you prefer a different type of rice, you can use brown rice, wild rice, or even orzo. Just adjust the cooking time as needed.
- **Vegetables:** Feel free to add other vegetables like bell peppers, green beans, or corn for extra nutrition and variety.

Enjoy your homemade Chicken and Rice Soup! It's a perfect meal to warm you up and keep you satisfied.

**Blackberry Cobbler**

## Ingredients

**For the Filling:**

- 4 cups fresh or frozen blackberries (if using frozen, do not thaw)
- 3/4 cup granulated sugar (adjust to taste, depending on the sweetness of the berries)
- 1 tablespoon lemon juice
- 1 tablespoon cornstarch
- 1/2 teaspoon vanilla extract

**For the Topping:**

- 1 cup all-purpose flour
- 1/4 cup granulated sugar
- 1/4 cup packed brown sugar
- 1 1/2 teaspoons baking powder
- 1/4 teaspoon salt
- 1/4 cup unsalted butter, cold and cut into small pieces
- 1/2 cup milk (whole milk or 2% is best)
- 1/2 teaspoon vanilla extract

## Instructions

1. **Preheat Oven:**
   - Preheat your oven to 375°F (190°C). Grease a 9-inch square baking dish or a similar-sized dish.
2. **Prepare the Filling:**
   - In a large bowl, gently toss the blackberries with granulated sugar, lemon juice, cornstarch, and vanilla extract. Let sit for about 10 minutes to allow the juices to combine and the cornstarch to thicken the mixture.
3. **Prepare the Topping:**
   - In a medium bowl, whisk together the flour, granulated sugar, brown sugar, baking powder, and salt.
   - Cut in the cold butter using a pastry cutter or your fingers until the mixture resembles coarse crumbs.
   - Stir in the milk and vanilla extract until just combined. The batter will be thick.
4. **Assemble the Cobbler:**
   - Pour the blackberry mixture into the prepared baking dish.
   - Drop spoonfuls of the topping batter over the blackberry filling. The topping will spread and cover the filling slightly, but it doesn't need to be perfect.
5. **Bake:**
   - Bake in the preheated oven for 35-40 minutes, or until the topping is golden brown and the filling is bubbling.
6. **Cool and Serve:**

- Allow the cobbler to cool for at least 15 minutes before serving. This helps the filling to set slightly.

## Tips:

- **Berry Variations:** Feel free to mix in other berries like raspberries or blueberries for a different twist.
- **Sweetness:** Adjust the sugar in the filling based on the tartness of the blackberries and your taste preference.
- **Topping Texture:** For a slightly sweeter and crispier topping, you can sprinkle a little extra granulated sugar on top before baking.

Serve your blackberry cobbler warm with a scoop of vanilla ice cream or a dollop of whipped cream for an extra treat. Enjoy!

**Sausage and Potato Hash**

## Ingredients

- 1 pound (450g) breakfast sausage (pork, turkey, or your choice), casings removed if necessary
- 1 pound (450g) potatoes, diced (Russet or Yukon Gold work well)
- 1 medium onion, chopped
- 1 red bell pepper, diced
- 2 cloves garlic, minced
- 1/2 teaspoon smoked paprika (optional, for extra flavor)
- 1/2 teaspoon dried thyme or rosemary (optional)
- Salt and black pepper, to taste
- 2 tablespoons olive oil or vegetable oil
- Fresh parsley, chopped (for garnish, optional)
- Eggs (optional, for serving; cooked to your preference)

## Instructions

1. **Prepare the Potatoes:**
   - In a large skillet or cast-iron pan, heat 1 tablespoon of oil over medium heat.
   - Add the diced potatoes and cook, stirring occasionally, until they are golden brown and tender, about 15-20 minutes. You may need to add a bit more oil if the potatoes are sticking. Transfer the cooked potatoes to a plate and set aside.
2. **Cook the Sausage:**
   - In the same skillet, add the remaining 1 tablespoon of oil. Crumble the sausage into the pan and cook over medium heat until browned and fully cooked, breaking it up into smaller pieces as it cooks.
3. **Add Vegetables:**
   - Add the chopped onion and diced red bell pepper to the skillet with the sausage. Cook for about 5 minutes, or until the onion is translucent and the pepper is tender.
   - Stir in the minced garlic and cook for another 1 minute, until fragrant.
4. **Combine and Season:**
   - Return the cooked potatoes to the skillet with the sausage and vegetables. Stir to combine.
   - Season with smoked paprika, dried thyme or rosemary (if using), salt, and black pepper. Cook for an additional 5 minutes, allowing the flavors to meld together.
5. **Serve:**
   - Garnish with chopped fresh parsley if desired. Serve the hash hot on its own or with eggs cooked to your liking (fried, poached, scrambled, etc.).

## Tips:

- **Potatoes:** For extra crispy potatoes, you can parboil them for a few minutes before sautéing, or use leftover cooked potatoes.
- **Sausage Variations:** Feel free to use different types of sausage, such as chorizo or Italian sausage, to change the flavor profile.
- **Additions:** You can add other vegetables like mushrooms, spinach, or zucchini for more variety and nutrition.

This Sausage and Potato Hash is a great base recipe that you can adapt to your tastes and what you have on hand. Enjoy your hearty and flavorful meal!

# Roasted Tomato and Basil Bruschetta

## Ingredients

- 1 pint cherry or grape tomatoes, halved
- 2 tablespoons olive oil
- 1/2 teaspoon salt
- 1/4 teaspoon black pepper
- 2 cloves garlic, minced
- 1/4 teaspoon dried oregano (optional)
- 1/4 teaspoon balsamic vinegar (optional, for added depth)
- 1/4 cup fresh basil leaves, chopped (plus extra for garnish)
- 1 French baguette or Italian bread, sliced into 1/2-inch thick slices
- Additional olive oil, for brushing the bread
- 1/4 cup grated Parmesan cheese (optional, for added flavor)

## Instructions

1. **Roast the Tomatoes:**
    - Preheat your oven to 400°F (200°C).
    - Arrange the halved tomatoes on a baking sheet. Drizzle with 2 tablespoons of olive oil, and sprinkle with salt, black pepper, minced garlic, and dried oregano if using.
    - Roast in the preheated oven for 20-25 minutes, or until the tomatoes are soft and caramelized. If using, drizzle with balsamic vinegar during the last 5 minutes of roasting.
2. **Prepare the Bread:**
    - While the tomatoes are roasting, preheat your oven to broil or use a grill.
    - Brush the bread slices lightly with olive oil on both sides.
    - Place the bread slices on a baking sheet and toast under the broiler or on a grill for about 1-2 minutes per side, or until golden brown and crispy. Watch carefully to avoid burning.
3. **Assemble the Bruschetta:**
    - Once the tomatoes are roasted and slightly cooled, stir in the chopped fresh basil.
    - Spoon the roasted tomato mixture onto the toasted bread slices.
    - If desired, sprinkle with grated Parmesan cheese for an extra touch of flavor.
4. **Garnish and Serve:**
    - Garnish with additional fresh basil leaves.
    - Serve immediately while the bread is still warm and crispy.

## Tips:

- **Tomato Variety:** Cherry or grape tomatoes work well because they roast nicely and have a sweet flavor. You can also use larger tomatoes; just cut them into smaller pieces and adjust the roasting time.
- **Bread Choice:** Use a crusty French baguette or Italian bread for the best texture. You can also use gluten-free or whole-grain bread if you prefer.
- **Make Ahead:** You can roast the tomatoes ahead of time and store them in the refrigerator for up to 3 days. Toast the bread just before serving to maintain its crispiness.

Enjoy your Roasted Tomato and Basil Bruschetta—it's a delightful and fresh appetizer that's sure to be a hit!

**Chocolate Chip Walnut Cookies**

## Ingredients

- 1 cup (2 sticks) unsalted butter, softened
- 1 cup granulated sugar
- 1 cup packed brown sugar
- 2 large eggs
- 1 teaspoon vanilla extract
- 3 cups all-purpose flour
- 1 teaspoon baking soda
- 1/2 teaspoon baking powder
- 1/2 teaspoon salt
- 1 1/2 cups semisweet chocolate chips
- 1 cup chopped walnuts

## Instructions

1. **Preheat Oven:**
   - Preheat your oven to 350°F (175°C). Line baking sheets with parchment paper or silicone baking mats.
2. **Cream Butter and Sugars:**
   - In a large bowl, using an electric mixer, beat the softened butter, granulated sugar, and brown sugar until light and fluffy.
3. **Add Eggs and Vanilla:**
   - Beat in the eggs one at a time, ensuring each is fully incorporated before adding the next. Mix in the vanilla extract.
4. **Combine Dry Ingredients:**
   - In a separate bowl, whisk together the flour, baking soda, baking powder, and salt.
5. **Mix Dry and Wet Ingredients:**
   - Gradually add the dry ingredients to the butter mixture, mixing on low speed until just combined.
6. **Fold in Chips and Walnuts:**
   - Stir in the chocolate chips and chopped walnuts until evenly distributed throughout the dough.
7. **Scoop Dough:**
   - Use a cookie scoop or tablespoon to drop rounded balls of dough onto the prepared baking sheets, spacing them about 2 inches apart.
8. **Bake:**
   - Bake in the preheated oven for 10-12 minutes, or until the edges are golden brown. The centers may still be soft; they will firm up as they cool.
9. **Cool:**

- Allow the cookies to cool on the baking sheets for a few minutes before transferring them to wire racks to cool completely.

## Tips:

- **Butter:** Ensure the butter is softened, but not melted, for the best cookie texture.
- **Mix-Ins:** Feel free to substitute or add other mix-ins like dried fruit, toffee bits, or different types of chocolate chips.
- **Storage:** Store cookies in an airtight container at room temperature for up to one week. They can also be frozen for up to 3 months. To freeze, place the cookies in a single layer on a baking sheet, freeze until solid, then transfer to a freezer bag or container.

Enjoy your homemade Chocolate Chip Walnut Cookies! They're a delightful combination of flavors and textures that are sure to please any cookie lover.

**Spiced Pear Compote**

## Ingredients

- 4 ripe pears, peeled, cored, and diced (Bosc, Anjou, or Bartlett pears work well)
- 1/2 cup granulated sugar
- 1/4 cup water (or apple juice for added flavor)
- 1/2 teaspoon ground cinnamon
- 1/4 teaspoon ground nutmeg
- 1/4 teaspoon ground ginger
- 1/4 teaspoon allspice (optional)
- 1 tablespoon lemon juice
- 1 teaspoon vanilla extract

## Instructions

1. **Prepare the Pears:**
   - Peel, core, and dice the pears into bite-sized pieces.
2. **Cook the Pears:**
   - In a medium saucepan, combine the diced pears, sugar, and water (or apple juice). Stir to combine.
   - Add the ground cinnamon, nutmeg, ginger, and allspice (if using). Stir well to coat the pears with the spices.
3. **Simmer:**
   - Bring the mixture to a gentle boil over medium heat. Reduce the heat to low and let it simmer, uncovered, for about 15-20 minutes, or until the pears are tender and the mixture has thickened to your desired consistency.
4. **Add Lemon Juice and Vanilla:**
   - Stir in the lemon juice and vanilla extract. Continue to cook for an additional 1-2 minutes.
5. **Cool and Serve:**
   - Remove from heat and let the compote cool slightly before serving. It can be served warm, at room temperature, or chilled.

## Tips:

- **Texture:** If you prefer a smoother compote, you can use a potato masher or fork to mash some of the pears as they cook. For a chunkier texture, leave the pears in larger pieces.
- **Spices:** Adjust the spices to your taste. You can also add a splash of brandy or a tablespoon of honey for additional flavor.
- **Storage:** Store any leftover compote in an airtight container in the refrigerator for up to a week. It can also be frozen for up to 3 months. To reheat, simply warm it up on the stovetop or in the microwave.

Enjoy your spiced pear compote as a delightful addition to your meals or as a standalone treat!

**Savory Herb Scones**

## Ingredients

- 2 cups all-purpose flour
- 1 tablespoon baking powder
- 1/2 teaspoon salt
- 1/2 teaspoon black pepper
- 1/4 teaspoon garlic powder (optional)
- 1/2 cup cold unsalted butter, cut into small pieces
- 1 cup shredded sharp cheddar cheese (or your favorite cheese)
- 1/4 cup chopped fresh herbs (such as chives, rosemary, thyme, or parsley)
- 3/4 cup buttermilk (or whole milk)
- 1 large egg
- Optional: 1 tablespoon milk for brushing the tops
- Optional: Extra shredded cheese or herbs for topping

## Instructions

1. **Preheat Oven:**
   - Preheat your oven to 400°F (200°C). Line a baking sheet with parchment paper or a silicone baking mat.
2. **Prepare Dry Ingredients:**
   - In a large bowl, whisk together the flour, baking powder, salt, black pepper, and garlic powder (if using).
3. **Cut in the Butter:**
   - Add the cold butter pieces to the flour mixture. Use a pastry cutter, fork, or your fingers to cut the butter into the flour until the mixture resembles coarse crumbs with pea-sized pieces of butter.
4. **Add Cheese and Herbs:**
   - Stir in the shredded cheese and chopped fresh herbs.
5. **Mix Wet Ingredients:**
   - In a separate bowl, whisk together the buttermilk and egg.
6. **Combine Ingredients:**
   - Pour the buttermilk mixture into the flour mixture. Stir gently until just combined; the dough will be slightly sticky. Do not overmix.
7. **Shape and Cut:**
   - Turn the dough out onto a lightly floured surface. Gently pat the dough into a 1-inch thick circle or rectangle. Use a knife or a round cutter to cut the dough into triangles or circles.
8. **Prepare for Baking:**
   - Transfer the cut scones to the prepared baking sheet. If desired, brush the tops with a little milk and sprinkle with additional shredded cheese or herbs.
9. **Bake:**

- Bake in the preheated oven for 15-20 minutes, or until the scones are golden brown and cooked through.
10. **Cool and Serve:**
    - Allow the scones to cool slightly on a wire rack before serving. Enjoy warm or at room temperature.

## Tips:

- **Cheese Varieties:** Experiment with different cheeses like Gruyère, Parmesan, or Gouda for varied flavors.
- **Herbs:** Fresh herbs add great flavor, but you can use dried herbs if fresh aren't available. Just reduce the amount to about 1 tablespoon of dried herbs.
- **Freezing:** You can freeze the unbaked scones. Place them on a baking sheet to freeze individually, then transfer to a freezer bag. Bake from frozen, adding a few extra minutes to the baking time.

These savory herb scones are sure to be a hit with anyone who enjoys a flavorful, flaky pastry. Enjoy!

www.ingramcontent.com/pod-product-compliance
Lightning Source LLC
LaVergne TN
LVHW081616060526
838201LV00054B/2271